Poems by an Aussie housewife

Tenea Dickinson

BookLeaf
Publishing

India | USA | UK

Presentation by *BookLeaf Publishing*

Web: www.bookleafpub.com

E-mail: info@bookleafpub.com

ISBN : 9789357447959

First edition 2021

DEDICATION

To Willie,

Being with you helps me understand poetry.

Whether or not it helps me write it remains to be seen.

My girls,

I don't worry so much about writing badly anymore because I have already created two of the most beautiful works of art imaginable.

Sylvie,

You're a good dog.

Stumpy,

You're an idiot.

PREFACE

Tenea is a twenty something stay at home mum
with infinite unfinished thoughts tangled
together in her yarn basket of a brain.
Perhaps you'll find some threads that match the
jumper you're knitting in your own mind.

Whispers in the Early Morning

Whispers in the early morning
Rocking bouncing patting yawning
Closing eyes
Lullabies
A new day is dawning

Together In That

He's been out there since sunrise
He's been running that horse round and round
He's training himself to train her

I've been tending to the kids
I've been watching through the window
I've been telling them their daddy is out doing
what he loves

And it's good if it helps him forget
And it's good if it fills his heart
And it's good that he has found something to
love even though it can't love him back

Cause at least
He and I are together
In that

On the Veranda with a Cuppa

The sun shines golden and the birds
they sing out!
And the pink of the rose is just so delightful
That my mind is enthralled by the beauty of its
performance
The gum leaf hangs lazily from the swaying
branch
It is doing just as it should
The yellow butterfly hastily pumps it's delicate
wings
But there is no stress despite the speed
And the blue sky
                      That intelligent blue
sky
Blissfully unaware
Effortless, casual
I refuse to despair

Yabbies in a Shell Pool

Trap is set
Yabby in a net

What a fool
Chucked in a kids pool

Nip your claw
In come more

Legs walk past
Better act fast

Pincers at the ready
Like you're gonna catch a netty

Lift 'em high
Like you're gonna stop a try

Clacking of thongs
Here come the tongs

Lifted in the air

Doesn't seem fair

Dropped in a pot
Boiling hot

Licking of lips
Served with chips

A Lie

If I could meet you all over
That warm, sneezy October
I'd hold out my hand and say
'Hello there, my name's Tenea'

Then simply be on my way

I Just Wish It Were Real

We LAUGH and CHAT and CHARM our guests
We DANCE and SING and KISS our kids
I have your name
That's all that's same
You sing about looooooove and my heart
whoooooooshes 'round

                              and I think that
maybe I could heal

You FISH while I READ and we CAMP by the
creek
We PLAY and CHASE and CATCH our girl
We cheers a beer
Hold the baby near
Domestic blissssss! Nothing better than
thissssss!

I just wish it were real

Just a Feeling

Feelings do not get the bill
Don't water my roses
Or my stomach fill

I can't touch them
Can't clutch them
Can't tack them up
Can't pack them up

Feelings aren't living here
They aren't knocking off on a Friday
Kicking back with a beer

They don't fix taps
They don't find caps
Won't heal a scratch
Won't sew a patch

Feelings don't know why they exist
Don't know what to do next
And yet they persist

At times I want them gone
Sometimes I want them torn
Nothing but the thinking leave

All but the body thieve

But without them I'm just not sure
Could my kids flourish
With my heart out the door?

Feelings can warm you up
Can fill a cup
They can hide you away
They can help you to stay

Its an uncomfortable truth
Feelings take up space
No, I don't have any proof
Or the time to waste

I just know that I'd rather
Be emotional and raw
then be robotic and without a flaw

How Spiders are Made

There are cobwebs on the ceiling
Around the lights
Near the paint that's peeling

at breakfast I saw a spider
Black and thick
A smaller one beside her

At lunch I noticed them again
One atop the other
More than just friends

At dinner I looked up once more
the big spider remains
The other lay still on the floor

100% flax linen worries

If I can just cover all the beds in linen sheets
Hang towels of green bamboo beside the bath
Sit plants with art in the living room
Maybe straighten my hair

 then perhaps
     the worries and
stress will
     D i s a p p e a r

Socialising

This morning I walked around the park by the
river.
I said 'hello' to everyone I passed
and by the time I got home
I felt like I'd had a whole conversation

Probably Just the Sniffles

Four Weetbix in a bowl
Sick baby on my hip
Past week taking a toll
Coffee cold without a sip

Vomit down my front
Playschool on repeat
Going on a sock hunt
Cover those cold little feet

The vacuum head breaks off
Soapy water in the sink
Can't seem to shake this cough
Internet's on the blink

Charlie and the chocolate factory we're readin'
four year old seems to be engaged
Dark chocolate she's eatin'
Asking for another page

She finishes her treat
She giggles with glee

I stop reading and our eyes meet
Then she asks to watch tv

Baby has to sleep in the pouch
Won't have a bar of her bed
The bags under my eyes can vouch
I tried what the book said

Sitting on a yoga ball
Snoring babe tied to my chest
Waiting for that magic phone call
With results from our Covid test

A Cold One in the Trenches

The rain dotted the dusty yard
The beer poured out and fizzed
The puzzles of life, so mind numbingly hard
For once they cease to quiz

Finger by finger my fist of a brain unclenches
No, not out of trouble yet
Just enjoying a cold one in the trenches

I May Not Look Like Marylin Monroe But Neither Do You

There's a hidden voice deep within
That says I'm as beautiful as Marylin
It whispers proudly of my curls
Of my teeth as white as pearls
It tells me that if I winked with my long dark
lashes
I would probably cause car crashes

But there's a another voice that says 'no'
You don't look a thing like Ms Monroe
It scoffs and says my legs are Stumpy
It scowls and declares my style frumpy
I should stay at home and save myself the
embarrassment
I just laugh at them both and so ends the
harassment

Why We Write

It's not about breaking through
Not about becoming well known
It's not about writing what's true
Not about an intellectual tone

It's not about proving that I'm deep
Not about showing my worth
It's not about making them weep
Not about expressing mirth

It's about plucking out something unseeable
About pinning down something untouchable
It's about airing out the unbreathable
About gripping onto the unclutchable

It's about seeing before us
A fragment of what we suspect lives within us

It Takes Guts to Bleed From Your Cuts

A broken heart is reason enough to be mean
Failure does ruin a day
Depression is a bad dream
Unrequited love, a bad way

But being nice when your glad
Doesn't take as much guts
As being kind when your sad
Bleed love from your cuts

Windsday

It doesn't break my heart anymore
It just reminds me that my heart is
scattered   around
   my   body   like
leaves

      after
                    a   big
   wind

Girl and Dog

Australia in the sun
Kelpies going for a run
Water in the paddock
Kid being dramatic
Wet from boot to cowboy hat
Alive from flat foot to long brown plait
Chasing the three legged dog
That everyone else thinks a flog
Tea party in the puddle
Girl and dog having a cuddle

The Perils of Being Unorganised

Where do all the socks go?
Into cracks and places down low
Where do all the dummies end up?
On the path and the back of the truck

Where does all the money flee?
Run back to that famous money tree
Where do all the dreams fly?
They form the clouds up in the sky

Where does the love run to?
Away from you away from you
Where does the pain come from?
It hitchhikes on every love song

Bathing in Merrin Creek

Baby on my lap
in the tray of the ute
  Radio blaring
  wind can't mute
Yodelling from Tex
    Better than sex
Who knew havin' a family was such a hoot!

We start moving backwards
she grabs hold of my knee
Bumping around
  House behind tree
  Squealing in fun
    Not quite one
Loving each thing her little eyes see

Akubra rests on RM's
 Nappy on the dirt
 Bra on a branch
    Phone under a shirt
    And with a thud
    Daddy's covered in mud

Strategically covering his Benjamin's

Blow brown bubbles
    my sweet little yabby
Kick your legs
  my little river cod
    Your safe with us
Remember to just
        Hold on tight to your daddy